How is the pattern of **life** ordered and followed?
How are **family** and marriage defined? How much sa...
How are manners, **etiquette**, and rules set? How flex...
To what degree is **education** emphasized? For both s...
How are **groups** created and identified? Which are m...
What **professions** dominate, and how is work viewed...
How is **information** gathered and spread?

Beauty   What is the **look most aspired to** in this group?
What are the contemporary **ideals** of male and female perfection?
What are the most **coveted** skin types, hair color and styles, and physical propor-
tions?
What part does physical **fitness** play in physical attractiveness? What is the rela-
tionship between beauty, health, and **comfort**?
Which **colors, shapes, textures,** and **silhouettes** are favored in clothing, furnish-
ings, props, hairdos, and jewelry?
How important is **fashion**? How fast does it **change**?
To what degree is **nature** altered to create a thing of beauty?
How is **taste** defined?
What are favored modes of **artistic expression**?

Sex   How significant a part of the collective **consciousness** is sex?
What do most people consider **turn-ons** and **turn-offs**?
How is **seduction** defined?
How is **sexuality** acceptably **communicated**? What are the sexual **stereotypes**?
Which parts of the **anatomy** are revealed, concealed, and emphasized?
Is the **emphasis** on the act or the chase? On pleasure or procreation?
What is the standard **courtship ritual** and its significance?
How much is **deviation** tolerated?
What are the accepted attitudes toward **infidelity** and **promiscuity**?
To what **degree** is sexuality **suppressed or expressed**?

Recreation   What is most people's idea of **fun**?
What would be an **ideal social occasion** in this world?
What is the **participation** level? Are they doers or watchers?
What is **intellectual** life? Are they thinkers or mindless hedonists?
What are the common **shared** hobbies, **pastimes**, and concepts of having fun?
What is most people's **vision** of an enjoyable evening, vacation, or day?
What are the differences between the **sexes**?
Consumption? What are the favored and coveted food, drink, drugs, and snacks?
What is the relative **importance** of recreation in life? The standard view of **indul-
gence**?

Sight   How do all the above manifest themselves in the way the world of the play looks,
in **shapes and angles, light** and **shadow, in dominant patterns**? In **standing, sit-
ting, facial expressions, ways of walking, touching,** and **being touched**?
What is the pattern of **movement** and **contact** and its significance?

Sound   How does it all come out in common **speech** and **nonverbal** communication?
To what degree are **listening** and **speaking** prized?
What is most desired in terms of **voice quality, timing, articulation, pronunciation,
use of pitch and volume, choice of words,** and **vocal patterns**?
What is the role of **music** and **dance** in life?

Style

FOR ACTORS